LE CORDON BLEU

HOME COLLECTION

·VEGETABLES·

PERIPLUS
EDITIONS

contents

recipe ratings ❋ *easy* ❋❋ *a little more care needed* ❋❋❋ *more care needed*

Vegetable pot-au-feu

A healthy, energizing dish that won't spoil your figure!
Simple to make and very satisfying.

*Preparation time **35 minutes***
*Total cooking time **1 hour 20 minutes***
Serves 6

STOCK
1 lb. chicken wings, disjointed
2 medium carrots, coarsely chopped
1 leek, coarsely chopped (see page 63)
2 stalks celery, coarsely chopped
1 onion, halved
2 whole cloves, inserted into the onion
1 bay leaf
3 sprigs of fresh thyme
2 carrots, cut into 1/4-inch cubes
2 turnips, cut into 1/4-inch cubes
1 lb. potatoes, cut into 1/4-inch cubes
2 cups trimmed and sliced green beans
1/2 cup frozen baby peas
2 tablespoons chopped fresh chervil
  or parsley, to garnish

1 To make the stock, put the chicken wings in a large saucepan and cover with about 3 quarts of water. Add the chopped carrots, leek, celery, onion halves and cloves, bay leaf and sprigs of thyme. Bring slowly to a boil, then reduce the heat and simmer for about 50 minutes. Skim frequently to remove any scum from the surface of the stock.

2 Pass the stock through a fine sieve. If possible, line the sieve with a piece of cheesecloth or a coffee filter paper to obtain a clear liquid. Discard the chicken, vegetables, herbs and spices.

3 Cook the cubed carrots, turnips and potatoes in boiling salted water for 2–3 minutes, or until tender but still crunchy. Plunge into cold water to stop the cooking process and keep the vegetables crunchy.

4 Cook the green beans in boiling salted water for 4 minutes. Drain, plunge into cold water to stop the cooking process and retain the green color, then drain again. Add the baby peas to boiling salted water and cook for 1 minute. Drain, plunge into cold water, then drain again.

5 Season the stock with salt and white pepper to taste. Add all the vegetables and reheat. Serve very hot in a soup dish and sprinkle with the chervil.

Rösti

A Rösti can be made from potatoes that have already been cooked, making a quick and delicious dish.

Preparation time **15 minutes**
Total cooking time **40 minutes**
Serves 6

‡

I lb. russet potatoes
oil, for cooking
I 1/2 tablespoons unsalted butter
I onion, thinly sliced

1 Preheat the oven to 350°F. Scrub the unpeeled potatoes and put them in a saucepan. Cover with cold water, add salt, and bring to a boil. Reduce the heat and simmer for 10 minutes. Drain and allow the potatoes to cool completely.
2 Peel the potatoes and either cut them into very thin sticks or coarsely shred them. Do not rinse.
3 In a nonstick ovenproof skillet, heat a little oil and add the butter. Gently cook the onion until soft and transparent. Add the potato, season with salt and pepper, mix for a few minutes, then press down with the back of a spoon or wide spatula to form a thick flat pancake. Brown one side over medium to high heat and transfer the pan to the oven for 15 minutes. Loosen and invert the pancake onto a large plate and then slide it off the plate and back into the pan browned-side-up. Be careful not to break the potatoes, and mind your fingers as there may be some loose hot oil and butter. Return to the oven and bake for another 10 minutes. For serving, cut into slices like a cake.

Artichokes with blue cheese

Tender artichoke bottoms or hearts are the most delicious part of this vegetable. Stuffing them with a blue cheese purée makes them extra special.

Preparation time **20 minutes**
Total cooking time **20 minutes**
Serves 4

‡ ‡

6 artichoke bottoms, cooked (see page 62)
I oz. blue cheese, crumbled
3 heaped tablespoons fresh bread crumbs
3 tablespoons unsalted butter, melted

1 Preheat the oven to 400°F. Rinse the cooked artichokes under cold water and set four aside.
2 Cut the remaining two artichokes into cubes and place in a food processor. Process with the crumbled blue cheese until smooth, then season with freshly ground black pepper. Spoon onto the four artichoke bottoms, shaping the purée into a dome. Place in a baking dish.
3 In a small bowl, mix the bread crumbs and half the butter together and sprinkle on top. Drizzle with the remaining melted butter and bake for 20 minutes, or until golden brown. In the picture, the artichokes are garnished with watercress.

Chef's tip If you cannot get fresh artichokes large enough for this recipe, good-quality preserved or canned ones work very well.

Rösti (top) and Artichokes with blue cheese

Crisp mushroom and chestnut pastries

A delicious combination of mushrooms and chestnuts with a light creamy sauce in crisp buttery pastry.
Serve as a first course or a light luncheon dish accompanied by a salad.

Preparation time **20 minutes + refrigeration**
Total cooking time **40 minutes**
Serves 4

2 sheets frozen puff pastry, thawed (see Chef's tips)
I egg, beaten
15 oz. mixed, wild mushrooms (see Chef's tips)
clarified butter (see page 63) or oil, for cooking
2 shallots, finely chopped
I clove garlic, crushed
juice of 1/2 lemon
2 tablespoons dry Madeira
2 oz. canned whole unsweetened
  chestnuts, coarsely chopped
1/2 cup chopped fresh parsley
1/2 cup heavy cream

1 Preheat the oven to 425°F. Brush each pastry sheet with water to barely moisten, fold in half lengthwise and gently press to seal. Cut each strip crosswise in half. Trim off the corners of each rectangle to shape a diamond and place diamonds on a damp baking sheet. Refrigerate for 20 minutes.
2 Brush the top surface of diamonds with beaten egg. Do not brush the sides as the egg will set and

prevent the pastry from rising. Bake for 15 minutes, or until crisp and golden brown. With a sharp knife, split the diamonds in half horizontally. Scrape out any soft dough and discard. Keep the pastry pieces warm.
3 To prepare the mushrooms, wash them two or three times, drain and cut into bite-size pieces. Heat a little clarified butter or oil in a large skillet and fry the mushrooms until golden brown. Drain, reserving the juices. Meanwhile, heat a little butter in a skillet and cook the shallots for 2–3 minutes. Add the garlic, lemon juice, Madeira, chestnuts and parsley. Season to taste.
4 Pour the mushroom juices into the shallot mixture and simmer, uncovered, until the liquid is reduced by half. Add the cream and season with salt and pepper. Reduce the sauce over high heat for 10 minutes, or until it is a syrupy consistency. Toss the mushrooms in the sauce and spoon into the bottom halves of the pastry. Arrange the pastry lids on top and serve.

Chef's tips Oyster, shiitake and chanterelle are all suitable mushrooms. Use one type or a mixture. If wild mushrooms are not available, use cultivated mushrooms, washing only once.

Pre-rolled frozen puff pastry can be purchased in 17 1/4 oz. packages, each containing two sheets, from gourmet or specialty food stores.

Potato and spinach croquettes

The humble, indispensable potato is enhanced with the flavors of spinach and Parmesan in these popular delights.

Preparation time **30 minutes**
Total cooking time **45 minutes**
Makes 14 croquettes

I lb. russet potatoes
pinch of ground nutmeg
I tablespoon unsalted butter
I egg yolk
oil, for deep- or pan-frying
1/3 cup freshly grated Parmesan
1/4 cup finely chopped cooked spinach
1/2 cup all-purpose flour, seasoned with salt
  and pepper
3 eggs, beaten
I tablespoon peanut oil
1 1/2 cups fine dry bread crumbs

1 Cut the potatoes into uniform pieces for even cooking, by halving or quartering, depending on their size. Put in a saucepan, cover with cold water and add a large pinch of salt. Bring to a boil, lower the heat and cook for at least 20 minutes, or until quite tender.

2 Drain the potatoes and dry them by shaking them in the pan over low heat for 2 minutes. Press them through a sieve or finely mash them until smooth. Season with salt and pepper to taste, and nutmeg. Add the butter and egg yolk. Spread out on a tray to cool. Preheat oil in a large saucepan, to 360°F. The oil will be hot enough when a cube of bread browns in 15 seconds.

3 Mix the Parmesan with the very well-drained spinach in a bowl. Add the potato, salt and pepper to this mixture and stir to combine. On a floured surface, and using floured hands, roll the mixture beneath a flat hand to form cylinders about 2 1/2 inches long and 3/4 inch wide. Even up and flatten the ends.

4 Place the seasoned flour on a plate. Combine the eggs and oil in a bowl and put the bread crumbs on a large piece of waxed paper. Roll the croquettes carefully through the flour and pat off the excess. Dip them in the egg to coat thoroughly, drain off the excess and roll in the bread crumbs, lifting the edges of the paper to make it easier. Sometimes it is necessary to coat the croquettes twice in the egg and crumbs. Do this if your mixture is a little too soft to hold its shape well. Fry in batches until evenly browned and lift out, shaking off any excess oil. Drain on crumpled paper towels.

Chef's tips The potato must not be too wet as the croquettes will split and absorb the oil.

Shake off or press on excess bread crumbs or they will burn and cling to the croquettes as unsightly specks.

Mediterranean-style roasted peppers

This colorful, tasty dish is suitable for serving as antipasto, as a first course or as a side dish with seafood, meat or chicken.

Preparation time **10 minutes + 3–4 hours marinating**
Total cooking time **10–15 minutes**
Serves 6

I red sweet bell pepper
I green sweet bell pepper
I yellow sweet bell pepper
2 teaspoons capers, finely chopped
4 canned anchovy fillets, finely chopped
4 tablespoons fresh basil leaves, shredded
¹/₃ cup olive oil

1 Cut all the peppers in half, remove the seeds and membranes and put the cut peppers on a broiler tray cut-side-down.
2 Brush the peppers with a little oil and cook under a preheated broiler until the skin has blackened and blistered. Cover with a tea towel or enclose in a plastic bag and allow the peppers to cool. The skins will then come away from the flesh more easily.
3 Remove the skins, cut the flesh into thick strips and put them in a bowl.
4 Place the capers, anchovies and basil in a jar, stir in the olive oil and pour the mixture over the peppers. Season to taste with salt and pepper. Marinate in the refrigerator for 3–4 hours before serving. Serve with focaccia and a green salad.

Eggplant caviar

*The name of this dish comes from the rather grainy appearance of the eggplant.
Delicious served with crisp Melba toast or warmed pita bread.*

*Preparation time **10 minutes + 1 hour refrigeration***
*Total cooking time **30 minutes***
Serves 6

1¹/₂ lb. eggplant
¹/₃ cup chopped pitted black olives
1 clove garlic, crushed
¹/₃ cup finely chopped fresh chives
²/₃ cup olive oil, plus extra for brushing
¹/₂ teaspoon sweet paprika

1 Preheat the oven to 350°F. Cut the eggplant in half lengthwise. Brush the cut sides with a little olive oil and sprinkle with salt and pepper. Place the halves cut-side-down in a baking dish or roasting pan.

2 Bake for 25–30 minutes, or until the flesh is very soft. Drain the eggplant to remove any liquid. Scrape out the flesh with a spoon, chop the flesh and put in a bowl.

3 Add the black olives, garlic and half the chives. Mix everything together using a fork, pressing the eggplant flesh against the sides of the bowl to break it down. Add the olive oil very slowly, stirring it into the mixture with the fork. Add the paprika and season to taste with salt and pepper. Refrigerate for 1 hour.

4 Spoon into a chilled bowl, sprinkle the top with the remaining chives and serve with Melba toast.

Chef's tip For a particularly special presentation, use two spoons to shape the mixture into small oval quenelles and arrange on individual plates. Sprinkle with chopped chives.

Braised red cabbage

The French name for this northern dish, an excellent accompaniment to roast pork or game, is chou rouge à la flamande. *Slow-cooking produces a wonderful result.*

*Preparation time **20 minutes***
*Total cooking time **1 hour 45 minutes***
Serves 8

1 red cabbage
3 tablespoons unsalted butter
1 onion, sliced
2 cooking apples
2¹/₂ tablespoons white wine vinegar
1 tablespoon sugar
2 tablespoons all-purpose flour

1 Preheat the oven to 325°F. Quarter the cabbage, cut out and discard the stalk and shred the cabbage finely. Put the cabbage in a large saucepan of boiling salted water (there should be enough water to more than cover the cabbage), bring back to a boil and drain. The cabbage will now have taken on an inky blue color. This is normal, and it will regain its color later. You may have to do this in batches, depending on the size of the saucepan.

2 Melt 1 tablespoon of the butter in a large flameproof casserole or Dutch oven, add the onion, cover and cook gently until transparent. Peel, quarter, core and slice the apples thinly before adding to the onion. Cook for a few minutes, then remove the mixture from the casserole.

3 Add the cabbage to the casserole, layering with the onion and apple mixture and sprinkling with the vinegar, sugar and 2 tablespoons of water. Season with salt and pepper. You will see the red color return as the vinegar is added. Cover with thickly buttered waxed paper and the lid and bake for about 1¹/2 hours, or until very tender. Stir occasionally and moisten with a little extra water if necessary.

4 Soften the remaining butter in a bowl and mix in the flour. Push the cabbage to one side of the pan. There will be some liquid at the bottom of the casserole. Add one quarter of the butter and flour and stir in. The liquid will thicken slightly. Repeat on the other side. Toss together and only add more butter and flour if any watery liquid is present. A lot of flavor and seasoning is in the liquid, so it is just thickened enough to cling to the cabbage. Taste and season. The cabbage should be gently sweet and sour. It may be necessary to add a little more sugar or vinegar, to taste.

Little stuffed vegetables

Master the preparation of these delightful, elegant vegetables so you and your friends can savor the results.

*Preparation time **45 minutes***
*Total cooking time **1 hour***
*Serves **4***

⚜

1 1/2 cups fresh bread crumbs
2/3 cup milk
olive oil, for cooking
4 oz. lean ground pork
4 oz. lean ground veal
3 cloves garlic, finely chopped
1 egg yolk, lightly beaten
2 1/2 tablespoons chopped fresh parsley
4 small turnips, about 2 inches in diameter
1 large zucchini, at least 8 1/2 inches in length,
  ends removed
2 large potatoes, peeled

1 Preheat the oven to 400°F. Mix the bread crumbs and milk in a large bowl and set aside while you cook the meat. In a large skillet, heat a little olive oil and cook the pork, veal and garlic for 5 minutes over medium heat. Remove from the heat and mix into the bread and milk. Season to taste with salt and pepper and add the egg and parsley. Set aside.

2 Peel the turnips and slice off the tops and bottoms, leaving the vegetables 1 1/2-inches high with a 1 1/2–2 inch diameter. Use a melon baller to scoop the flesh out. Discard the flesh, leaving a border 1/2-inch thick on the sides and bottom. Cut the zucchini into lengths, about 1 1/2 inches each, and scoop the flesh out, as with the turnips.

3 Cut the potatoes into 1 1/2-inch cubes and, using a 1 1/2-inch round biscuit or cookie cutter, cut the potatoes into round tubes. Scoop out the center as for the other vegetables. Blanch each vegetable in a separate pan of boiling water, being careful not to overcook any of them. They should remain firm.

4 Transfer the turnips and zucchini to a bowl of iced water and, when completely cooled, place upside down on paper towels to drain. When the potatoes are cooked, put them on paper towels, right-side-up, until cool enough to handle.

5 Season the interiors of the prepared vegetables and spoon the filling into them. Place the filled vegetables in a lightly oiled baking dish and brush with a little olive oil.

6 Bake for 20–30 minutes, or until just tender. If desired, brown under a broiler. You can serve this dish either hot or cold.

Vegetable strudel

A delightful start to a meal or perfect as a light luncheon dish. A slight hint of curry flavor enhances the lightly cooked vegetables in crisp pastry.

*Preparation time **40 minutes***
*Total cooking time **1 hour***
Serves 4–6 (Makes 10)

oil, for cooking
1 onion, chopped
1/2 teaspoon mild curry powder
3 cups mixed peeled vegetables,
 such as finely diced carrot, parsnip, turnip
 and celery root; green beans, cut into short
 lengths; tiny florets of cauliflower and broccoli;
 thinly sliced leek (see page 63)
2 1/2 tablespoons fresh bread crumbs
20 sheets phyllo pastry
oil or melted butter, for brushing

TOMATO AND CILANTRO SAUCE
1 tablespoon unsalted butter
1 onion, thinly sliced
1 lb. tomatoes, peeled, seeded and quartered
 (see page 62)
 or 16-oz. can tomato purée
1/4 cup vegetable or chicken stock (see page 63)
1 bay leaf
1 sprig of fresh thyme
4 tablespoons chopped fresh cilantro leaves

1 Preheat the oven to 375°F. Heat a little oil in a skillet or wok and gently fry the onion until just soft. Add the curry powder and blend in. Add the carrot, parsnip, turnip and celery root and toss for 2 minutes over high heat. Add the green beans, cauliflower and leek and toss for another minute before adding the broccoli and frying for 2 minutes. Transfer to a large bowl, lightly mix in the bread crumbs and season with salt and pepper to taste.

2 Brush one sheet of phyllo pastry with oil or melted butter and place another sheet on top before brushing again with oil or melted butter. Fold in half and scatter on the vegetables, leaving 1 inch on each long side free of filling. Turn these sides in and roll up the strudel carefully from one short end. Repeat this process until all the phyllo pastry and vegetables have been used. Transfer the strudels to a lightly buttered baking sheet and gently brush the pastry with oil or melted butter. Bake for 15–20 minutes, or until crisp and golden brown.

3 To make the tomato and cilantro sauce, melt the butter in a saucepan, add the onion and cook for 10 minutes until transparent. Add the tomatoes, stock, bay leaf and thyme, and season with salt and pepper. Bring to a boil, reduce the heat, cover and simmer for up to 20 minutes, or until rich and pulpy. Remove from the heat. Discard the bay leaf and thyme, add the cilantro and season to taste with salt and pepper. A pinch of sugar may be required if the tomatoes are sharp. Serve the strudels immediately with the tomato and cilantro sauce alongside.

Chef's tips The strudels should be served as soon as they are cooked, otherwise the pastry may go soft. If you prefer, prepare the strudels a few hours ahead and brush again with melted butter just before baking.

  This is an excellent recipe to use up small amounts of fresh vegetables in your refrigerator. Be careful not to use vegetables that will become watery and make the pastry soggy, such as zucchini. If using up cooked vegetables, dice them and mix in after cooking the onion, but do not cook further.

Roasted parsnips with honey and ginger

A very popular vegetable in Ancient Greece and during the Middle Ages and the Renaissance, the parsnip has a lovely sweet flavor.

Preparation time **10 minutes**
Total cooking time **20 minutes**
Serves 6

1 1/2 lb. parsnips
1/4 cup oil
1 tablespoon unsalted butter
1 tablespoon clear honey
1 tablespoon finely grated or chopped
   fresh ginger root

1   Preheat the oven to 425°F. Peel and cut the parsnips in half lengthwise, or quarters if they are large, to make pieces about 3 inches long and 1 inch thick. Remove any woody cores. Put in a large saucepan and cover with water. Add a pinch of salt and bring to a boil over high heat. Boil for 1 minute before draining. Return to the saucepan and dry well by shaking the pan over low heat for about 1 minute.
2   Heat the oil in a roasting pan on the stove top. Add the parsnips and cook quickly over high heat, turning to color evenly. Add the butter to the pan, transfer to the oven to roast for 10 minutes. Spoon out the excess oil.
3   Add the honey and ginger root, turning the parsnips to coat evenly, and roast for another 5 minutes.
4   Lift the parsnips out of the pan and serve hot with pork or chicken.

Baked eggplant

The pronounced flavor of the eggplant is often combined with tomato, garlic and herbs. These stuffed eggplants originated in Turkey as Imam bayildi.

*Preparation time **40 minutes***
*Total cooking time **1 hour***
Serves 4

olive oil, for cooking
2 large shallots, finely chopped
1 1/2 lb. tomatoes, peeled, seeded
  and diced (see page 62)
6 cloves garlic, finely chopped
small pinch of cayenne pepper
1 cup chopped fresh basil leaves
2 small eggplant
4 small tomatoes, stems removed
1 cup shredded Gruyère or Swiss cheese

1 Preheat the oven to 300°F. In a heavy-bottomed skillet, heat a little oil over medium heat, add the shallots and cook for 2–3 minutes, without coloring. Add the diced tomato and garlic, season with salt and cayenne pepper and simmer for 15 minutes, or until thick. Mix in the chopped basil, set aside and keep warm.

2 Meanwhile, cut the eggplant in half lengthwise. Score the flesh, being careful not to cut through the skin. Rub the surface with olive oil and season with salt. Place the eggplant cut-side-down in a baking dish and bake for 15 minutes, or until soft. Allow to cool. Increase the temperature of the oven to 400°F.

3 Cut the small tomatoes in half from top to bottom and thinly slice into semicircles. Set aside.

4 Carefully scoop out the flesh of the cooked eggplant. Set the empty skins aside. Chop up the pulp and remove some of the liquid by cooking in a skillet for 5–10 minutes over low heat. Transfer the eggplant pulp to a bowl and mix in half of the cooked tomato. Season and then spoon the mixture into the eggplant skins. Return the filled eggplant to the baking dish and arrange the tomato slices on top. Sprinkle with the shredded cheese and bake until golden brown.

5 Purée the remaining cooked tomato in a blender. Dilute if necessary with some water or chicken stock. Place in a small saucepan and heat through, checking the seasoning. To serve, spoon some of the tomato sauce onto the plate and arrange the eggplant on top.

Cauliflower mornay

*Perfect partners, cauliflower and cheese sauce baked in this way make a hearty winter
dish that never has the experience of being a leftover.*

*Preparation time **10 minutes***
*Total cooking time **30 minutes***
Serves 4–6

I whole cauliflower, about I lb. when trimmed
2 tablespoons unsalted butter
1/4 cup all-purpose flour
2 cups milk
pinch of ground nutmeg
1/3 cup whipping cream
I cup shredded Gruyère cheese
2 egg yolks

1 Preheat the oven to 350°F. Remove the outer leaves
of the cauliflower and break the head into large florets.
Place in cold salted water, bring slowly to a boil, reduce
the heat and simmer for about 10 minutes, or until the
cauliflower is cooked, but still slightly firm. Drain,
refresh in cold water, then drain again.
2 To make the cheese sauce, melt the butter in a
saucepan, stir in the flour with a wooden spoon or whisk
and cook over low heat for 3 minutes. Remove from the
heat and gradually stir in the cold milk. Return to the
heat and bring to a boil, stirring constantly. Add the
nutmeg and season with salt and pepper. Stir in the
cream. Remove from the heat and add 3/4 cup of the
cheese and the egg yolks. Set aside. Cover the surface
with plastic wrap or damp waxed paper to prevent a
skin from forming.
3 Lightly brush a baking dish with butter. Pour a thin
layer of the sauce into the dish, arrange the cauliflower
on the sauce and pour over the remaining sauce so that
it coats the cauliflower. Sprinkle with the remaining
cheese and some pepper and nutmeg and bake for
15 minutes, or until the cheese is golden brown.

Chef's tips If the sauce looks lumpy before the cream
has been added to it, simply whisk it until smooth. It is
important to do this before the cheese is added to
prevent strands of cheese from sticking to the whisk.

Gruyère is a strong cheese, but if you use a different
type with less strength, add a little mustard to bring out
the flavors.

Asparagus with hollandaise sauce

Before World War I, hollandaise sauce was called Sauce Isigny, after a town in Normandy known for its butter. During the war, butter production came to a halt and it was imported from Holland. The name was changed to hollandaise to indicate the source of the butter and was never changed back.

Preparation time **45 minutes**
Total cooking time **35 minutes**
Serves 4

HOLLANDAISE SAUCE
3 egg yolks
2/3 cup clarified butter, melted
   (see page 63)
small pinch of cayenne pepper
juice of 1/2 lemon

32 asparagus spears
1/3 cup kosher or coarse salt

1 To make the hollandaise sauce, whisk the egg yolks with 4 tablespoons of water in the top of a double boiler until foamy. Place over simmering water and continue whisking over low heat until the mixture is thick and you can see the trail made by the whisk. Remove the top pan from the heat and gradually add the butter, whisking constantly. Once all the butter has been incorporated, strain the sauce and season with salt to taste, a dash of cayenne pepper and the lemon juice. Keep the sauce warm over warm water. (If preferred, a food processor can be used to make the sauce. Whisk the egg yolks and water and, with the motor running, add the melted warm butter to the processor in a thin stream.)

2 Bring a large pan of water to a boil. Use a vegetable peeler to remove the outer layer from the lower two thirds of the stem of each asparagus spear. Line up the spears of asparagus and tie into bundles of eight.

3 Add the kosher or coarse salt and then the asparagus bundles to the water. Reduce the heat and simmer for 10 minutes, or until the tips are tender. Remove and drain on paper towels. Remove the string and arrange each bundle on a warm serving plate. Coat with some of the hollandaise sauce and serve immediately.

Chef's tip Hollandaise sauce is an emulsion like mayonnaise, but made with warm clarified butter, which helps to make a smooth sauce. Once made, the sauce should be kept lukewarm. If the sauce is overheated, it will separate. If this should happen, the sauce can be repaired by adding a little cold water and whisking.

Ratatouille

This is a classic dish from the sunny area of Provence using the freshest tomatoes, zucchini, eggplant, sweet peppers and onions, sautéed in olive oil with herbs.

*Preparation time **40 minutes***
*Total cooking time **1 hour***
Serves 4

1 onion, diced
¹/₃ cup olive oil, for cooking
4 tomatoes, peeled, seeded
  and chopped (see page 62)
2 cloves garlic, chopped
1 red sweet bell pepper, seeded and cut
  into short strips
bouquet garni (see Chef's tips)
2 zucchini, cut into batons
  (see page 63)
2 eggplants, cut into batons
1 cup chopped fresh basil leaves

1 Preheat the oven to 350°F. In a flameproof casserole or Dutch oven, cook the onion in a little of the olive oil, over medium-low heat, for 3–5 minutes, or until soft, being careful not to let the onion color. Add the tomato and garlic and cook for 15 minutes, stirring occasionally.

2 In a skillet, sauté the red pepper in oil for 2–3 minutes over medium-high heat. Strain off the excess oil and add to the tomato mixture with the bouquet garni.

3 Sauté the prepared zucchini and eggplant separately in oil, for 3–4 minutes. Add to the tomato mixture. Season with salt and pepper to taste, cover with a lid or foil and bake for 30 minutes. Just before serving, remove the bouquet garni, stir in the chopped fresh basil leaves and adjust the seasoning, if necessary.

Chef's tips The bouquet garni is a selection of herbs tied in a neat bundle for easy removal from the dish before serving. It is made by wrapping the green part of a leek around celery leaves, a sprig of thyme, a bay leaf and parsley stalks, and then securing them together with string. When using a herb such as basil in the recipe, you can replace the parsley stalks with the basil stalks for added flavor.

Provençal stuffed tomatoes

Olive oil, garlic, parsley and tomato predominate in the cuisine of the Provence region, reflecting its close proximity to Italy.

Preparation time **30 minutes + 20 minutes draining**
Total cooking time **15 minutes**
Serves 4

4 tomatoes
1/4 cup extra virgin olive oil
4 cloves garlic, finely chopped
1 tablespoon chopped fresh thyme leaves
2 tablespoons chopped fresh parsley
3/4 cup fresh bread crumbs

1 Preheat the oven to 375°F. Remove the stem ends from the tomatoes. Place the tomatoes stem-side-down (to make the tomatoes more secure) and cut in half. Carefully remove the seeds with a teaspoon. Season with some salt and leave, cut-side-down, on paper towels to drain for about 20 minutes.
2 Gently heat the olive oil until warm. Remove from the heat and add the garlic, thyme, parsley and bread crumbs. Season with salt and pepper and mix well using a wooden spoon. Season the tomato halves with pepper and fill with the bread stuffing, making a slight dome on top of each tomato half. Place in an oiled baking dish and drizzle with some extra olive oil. Bake for 5–10 minutes, or until the stuffing is golden.

Chef's tip This recipe would also work successfully using eight small tomatoes with the tops cut off and the seeds scooped out.

Mixed glazed vegetables

This colorful, attractively prepared mixture of vegetables looks very appealing presented at the table in a shallow dish.

*Preparation time **40 minutes***
*Total cooking time **30 minutes***
Serves 4

☼ ☼

20 small boiling onions
2 zucchini
3 turnips
3 carrots
1/4 cup unsalted butter
1 tablespoon sugar

1 Soak the boiling onions in a bowl of warm water for 5 minutes, to make peeling easier. Lightly trim the root end, being careful not to cut off too much, since it is the root end that will keep the onions intact.

2 Using a standard 3/4 inch melon baller, make 20 balls each of the zucchini, turnips and carrots. Cook the zucchini balls for 1 minute in boiling salted water and refresh in iced water. Drain and transfer to a small saucepan. Add one third of the butter, 1 teaspoon of the sugar, 1/2 teaspoon salt and 2 tablespoons water and cook until the water has evaporated and a syrupy glaze remains. Check to see if the vegetables are tender. If not, add some water and cook a little longer. Roll the vegetables around to evenly coat, then set aside and keep warm.

3 Put the turnip and carrot balls together in a pan with half of the remaining butter, 1 teaspoon of the sugar, 1/2 teaspoon salt and enough water to just cover. Cook in the same way as the zucchini, then set aside and keep warm. Repeat with the peeled onions.

4 Reheat by combining the vegetables in a pan, placing the pan over medium heat and rolling the vegetables around to prevent them from browning, for about 3–5 minutes. Transfer to a serving dish.

Chef's tips Leave the vegetables at room temperature for about 1 hour before preparing.

If you can't get boiling onions, use small brown or white onions and remove a few outer layers.

Chickpea and sesame fritters with garlic and olive sauce

Chickpeas feature in many dishes in the south of France, as well as in the Middle East and Spain.
These fritters team well with the garlicky flavor of the sauce.

Preparation time 55 minutes + 30 minutes soaking
Total cooking time 2 hours
Makes 20

3/4 cup dried chickpeas (garbanzos)
1/3 cup sesame oil
2 eggs, beaten
3/4 cup sesame seeds
oil, for deep-frying

GARLIC AND OLIVE SAUCE
1/2 head of garlic, separated into cloves
   and peeled
1 tablespoon unsalted butter
1/2 onion, chopped
3/4 cup milk
1/4 cup whipping cream, optional
2/3 cup black olives, chopped

1 tablespoon chopped fresh flat-leaf parsley or
   fresh cilantro leaves, optional

1 Soak the chickpeas in warm water for 30 minutes. Drain, cover well with fresh water in a saucepan and simmer for about 1 1/2 hours, or until soft.
2 Drain the chickpeas and while hot, purée them in a food processor until fine. Slowly incorporate the sesame oil. Season with salt and pepper to taste.
3 Roll the mixture into balls about the size of a soup spoon. Dip them in the beaten egg and coat with the sesame seeds. Heat the oil to 360°F, and deep-fry the balls in batches until golden. Drain on paper towels and keep warm.
4 To make the garlic and olive sauce, gently sauté the garlic in the butter until golden brown. Add the onion and cook until the onion is just soft but without color. Add the milk, bring to a boil and cook for 10 minutes. Purée the mixture in a blender, add the cream, and salt and pepper to taste. Strain the sauce and add the chopped black olives.
5 Place three or four of the chickpea fritters per person on plates and pour the garlic and olive sauce around them. Sprinkle with the chopped fresh parsley or cilantro leaves and serve immediately.

Vegetable tian

Layers of vegetables with added flavor from herbs and garlic are delicious baked in a shallow casserole that can be presented at the table. Suitable for lunch or dinner.

Preparation time **30 minutes**
Total cooking time **1 hour**
Serves 4

olive oil, for cooking
1 small onion, thinly sliced
1 1/2 lb. tomatoes, peeled,
    seeded and diced (see page 62)
2 portobello mushrooms, thinly sliced
4 potatoes, thinly sliced
2 cloves garlic, finely chopped
1 lb. spinach leaves,
    stems removed
1 sprig of fresh rosemary
1/4 cup chopped fresh parsley

1 Preheat the oven to 375°F. In a heavy-bottomed skillet, heat a little olive oil over medium heat and gently cook the sliced onion with a pinch of salt for 3 minutes, without allowing to color. Add the seeded and diced tomato and cook gently for 7 minutes. Season to taste, transfer to a bowl and set aside.

2 Sauté the mushrooms in a little olive oil over high heat for 3–4 minutes. Drain off any excess moisture. Season to taste, remove and set aside.

3 Sauté the potatoes in batches in some olive oil, over medium-low heat for 3 minutes. Return all the potatoes to the pan, add the garlic and cook for another minute. Season with salt and freshly ground black pepper and drain on paper towels.

4 Arrange a layer of potatoes in the bottom of a 2-quart, 8-inch-diameter round or oval baking dish and cover with a layer of the mushrooms, followed by a layer of spinach, then a layer of tomatoes. Bake for 30–45 minutes, covered with waxed paper. Sprinkle with rosemary leaves and parsley before serving.

Chef's tip If desired, cover the vegetables with grated Parmesan or crumbled feta cheese before baking.

Celery root rémoulade

This is a delicious first course or it can be served as a light lunch, perhaps with chunks of bread. The mustardy mayonnaise enhances the crunchy, unique taste of celery root.

Preparation time **40 minutes**
   + 30–60 minutes resting
Total cooking time **None**
Serves **4–6**

※

2–3 celery roots, total weight about 2¹/₂ lb.
juice of I lemon
several small salad leaves, to garnish
2 tomatoes, peeled, seeded and diced
  (see page 62), to garnish
walnut halves, to garnish

REMOULADE SAUCE
2 egg yolks
2¹/₂ tablespoons Dijon mustard
pinch of cayenne pepper
I cup peanut oil

1 Using a large knife, cut each celery root in half and peel away the skin, cutting about ¹/₈ inch deep under the skin (the skin is very fibrous so it is important to cut off enough). Coarsely shred the celery root and put the flesh in a bowl. Season with salt and pepper and toss in the lemon juice. Cover with plastic wrap and set aside for 30–60 minutes.

2 To make the rémoulade sauce, in a medium bowl, whisk together the egg yolks, mustard, cayenne pepper and a pinch of salt. Once the salt has dissolved, gradually whisk in the oil. The sauce should resemble stiffly whipped cream.

3 Squeeze out the excess liquid from the shredded celery root and mix the celery root with the sauce. Season with salt and freshly ground black pepper, if necessary. Serve the rémoulade in a large bowl or in small mounds on individual plates, decorated with the salad leaves, tomatoes and walnuts.

Stuffed cabbage

This is an excellent luncheon or supper dish. In some countries, cabbage is not regarded as a vegetable suitable for serving as a separate course, but the following is definitely worthy of being offered in this way.

Preparation time **45 minutes**
Total cooking time **1 hour 35 minutes**
Serves 6

1 green cabbage, about 1–1 1/2 lb.
1/4 cup unsalted butter
1 small onion, finely chopped
1 1/2 cups fresh bread crumbs
1/3 cup chopped fresh parsley
1 tablespoon chopped fresh thyme leaves
grated rind of 1/2 lemon
2 eggs, beaten
1 tablespoon clarified butter (see page 63)
tomato pureé, seasoned, to serve

1 Trim off any tired cabbage leaves, but leave the cabbage whole. Plunge it into a large saucepan of boiling water. Boil for 3–4 minutes. Pour off the hot water, transfer the cabbage to a colander and drain well. Allow to cool slightly. Carefully remove four to six outside leaves and set aside. Cut the cabbage into quarters, remove the stalk, then slice the cabbage and chop finely.

2 Melt the butter in a large saucepan, add the onion, cover and cook gently for 1–2 minutes. Add the cabbage, press a piece of buttered waxed paper on the top, cover the pan and cook over low heat for 25–30 minutes, stirring thoroughly once or twice during cooking. The cabbage should be soft and golden all through. Remove from heat, stir in 1 cup of the bread crumbs, the herbs, lemon rind and eggs, and season with salt and pepper.

3 Line a large mixing bowl with a buttered piece of cheesecloth. Arrange the reserved outside leaves in this, stalks upright. Fill with the mixture, gather the ends of the cloth tightly, twist and tie the cloth to give the cabbage a plump shape. Lift out of the bowl, and plunge the cabbage into a pan of boiling salted water or vegetable stock. Boil gently and steadily for 45 minutes to 1 hour. Turn it over once or twice during cooking. Lift out into a colander, drain well, untie the cloth and turn the cabbage over onto a heated dish.

4 Melt the clarified butter in a small skillet, add the remaining bread crumbs and fry until golden. Sprinkle over the cabbage and serve at once with the well-seasoned tomato purée poured around.

Green beans with bacon

*Very popular as a vegetable on the side, served with broiled or roasted meats or chicken.
The salty flavor of bacon blends perfectly with green beans.*

*Preparation time **10 minutes***
*Total cooking time **15 minutes***
Serves 4–6

1 lb. green or yellow wax beans
1 teaspoon salt
10 oz. bacon
1/4 cup unsalted butter
1/4 cup finely chopped fresh parsley

1 Trim the beans. Bring a large saucepan of water to a boil. Add the salt and the beans and simmer for 10 minutes, or until tender. Drain and refresh in cold water to stop the cooking process. Drain well.
2 Meanwhile, remove any rind from the bacon and discard. Cut the bacon into small, short strips. Heat a skillet, add the bacon and fry over medium heat. There is no need to add any fat, the bacon's own fat will melt into the pan as it cooks. Remove the bacon and drain on paper towels.
3 Drain the excess fat from the pan, wipe with paper towels and then melt the butter in the pan. Toss the beans in the butter, add the bacon and season with salt and pepper. As soon as they are warmed through, transfer to a serving dish, sprinkle with chopped parsley and serve.

Chef's tips To maintain the green color of the beans, simultaneously throw the salt and the beans into the boiling water. This creates a fast bubble, which helps to fix the chlorophyll.

As a variation, substitute the bacon with two or three canned anchovy fillets. Prepare them first by soaking in milk, draining and then drying them. Finely chop them and toss in the butter.

Gratin dauphinois

This potato dish has many versions, some with onion or other vegetables added, some with stock and different herbs. Seasoning, cheese, cream and garlic are the key to making this particular version successful. Experiment to suit your own taste.

*Preparation time **30 minutes***
*Total cooking time **1 hour***
*Serves **4–6***

1 lb. potatoes
2 cups milk
nutmeg, freshly grated
¹/3 cup heavy cream
1 clove garlic, finely chopped
1 cup shredded Swiss cheese

1 Preheat the oven to 325°F.
2 Thinly slice the potatoes. Place in a saucepan, cover with the milk and season with some salt, pepper and grated nutmeg.
3 Bring to a simmer over medium-low heat and simmer until the potato is almost cooked but still firm. Strain and set the milk aside.
4 Rub an 8 x 6¹/2-inch oblong baking dish with some butter. Arrange the potatoes in even layers in the dish.
5 Reheat the milk and allow to simmer for a few minutes. Add the cream and garlic, bring back to a simmer and check the seasoning. Simmer for a few minutes, then pour over the potatoes. Sprinkle with the shredded cheese and bake for 35–45 minutes, or until the potatoes are tender and the top is lightly browned.

Chef's tip When making a sauce to accompany a bland vegetable such as potatoes, be sure to season it well.

Vichy carrots

The water used for cooking this dish should really be Vichy water, a natural and healthy mineral water from the springs at Vichy in France. These carrots are a colorful accompaniment to veal and chicken dishes.

Preparation time **15–20 minutes**
Total cooking time **20–30 minutes**
Serves 4

1 1/4 lb. carrots
2 tablespoons sugar
1/4 cup unsalted butter
1/2 cup chopped fresh parsley

1 Peel the carrots, slice thinly and put in a pan with enough water to barely cover. Add a pinch of salt as well as the sugar and butter and cover with a paper lid made from a round of waxed paper (see Chef's tips).
2 Cook over high heat until almost all the water has evaporated, leaving a syrupy reduction. The carrots should be tender. If not, add a little more water (about

1/4 cup) and continue cooking. Toss the carrots with the butter to evenly coat them. Sprinkle with the chopped fresh parsley and serve in a deep dish.

Chef's tips Cut the carrots into different shapes to make a more decorative and attractive presentation.

A paper lid serves to slow the process of steam escaping, allowing foods to remain moist and prevent them from cooking too quickly. To make a paper lid, prepare a piece of waxed paper larger than the diameter of the pan. Fold in half, then in quarters and fold once again into a fan shape. To measure the diameter of the pan, place the point in the center of the pan and cut at the point the folded paper reaches the edge of the pan. Snip off the point and unfold. The paper should now be a circle about the same diameter as the pan with a small hole in the center.

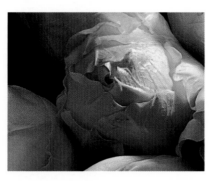

Braised Belgian endive

*A vegetable that is wonderful braised, even though it is often thought
of as being a salad ingredient.*

*Preparation time **15 minutes***
*Total cooking time **1 hour 30 minutes***
Serves 4

1/4 cup unsalted butter
4 Belgian endives
2 cups chicken stock
  (see page 63) or water
1 tablespoon lemon juice
1/2 teaspoon sugar
1 teaspoon chopped fresh parsley

1 Preheat the oven to 350°F. Grease a flameproof casserole with one third of the butter. Remove any blemished outer leaves of the endives and trim and core the root ends. This removes some of the bitterness. Wash and place them in the casserole.

2 Add the chicken stock or water to the casserole with the lemon juice. Season lightly with salt, pepper and the sugar. Bring to a boil on the stove top. Remove and cover with buttered waxed paper and then foil or a lid. Transfer to the oven and bake for about 1–11/4 hours, or until the endives are tender. Remove the endives and place on a rack to drain, reserving the cooking liquid. Cook the liquid over high heat until syrupy. Set aside and keep warm.

3 Once the endives are cooled, lightly tie in the middle with some kitchen string. Heat the remaining butter in a nonstick skillet and brown the endives until they are nicely colored. Remove the string, place the endives in a serving dish and cover with the reduced cooking liquid. Sprinkle with the parsley.

Chef's tip Before tying with the string, you can wrap a slice of bacon around the middle.

Barbecued marinated vegetables

Served cold with a vinaigrette or hot straight from the grill, these vegetables make a delicious light dish, full of color and flavor.

*Preparation time **20 minutes + 2 hours marinating***
*Total cooking time **40 minutes***
Serves 6

❋ ❋

1 eggplant
2. zucchini
2 carrots
3 red sweet bell peppers
9 button mushrooms, washed
2 sprigs of fresh thyme, finely chopped
2 sprigs of fresh parsley, finely chopped
2/3 cup olive oil
1 tablespoon freshly squeezed lemon juice
1/4 cup chopped fresh basil
3 tablespoons balsamic vinegar

1 Cut the eggplant, zucchini and carrots lengthwise into long slices, about 1/2 inch thick. Halve the peppers, remove the seeds and halve into quarters. Remove the mushroom stems.

2 Spread the vegetables on a tray, sprinkle with salt and pepper, the thyme and parsley. Reserve 2 tablespoons of the olive oil and combine the rest with the lemon juice. Pour over the vegetables and sprinkle with the basil. Marinate for 2 hours.

3 Heat a barbecue or broiler and brush the rack or broiler tray with the reserved oil. Slowly cook the vegetables on both sides until tender. (If you prefer less crunchy carrots, cook them for a few minutes before adding the other vegetables.)

4 Arrange the vegetables on a dish and drizzle with the balsamic vinegar.

Vegetable lasagna

Try this deliciously different lasagna with its crunchy vegetables and cheese sauce with a hint of nutmeg. Making your own pasta is both enjoyable and satisfying.

Preparation time 1 hour + 30 minutes resting
Total cooking time 1 hour 30 minutes
Serves 6

PASTA DOUGH
2 1/2 cups all-purpose flour
3 eggs, lightly beaten
2 tablespoons olive oil
1 teaspoon salt

CHEESE SAUCE
1 1/2 tablespoons unsalted butter
3 tablespoons all-purpose flour
2 cups milk
1/4 teaspoon ground nutmeg
1/4 cup whipping cream
1 cup shredded Gruyère cheese

TOMATO SAUCE
1 1/2 tablespoons unsalted butter
1 small onion, sliced
4 ripe tomatoes, peeled, seeded
    and chopped (see page 62)
1 sprig of fresh thyme
1 bay leaf
1 1/4 cups diced carrots
3 1/3 cups small broccoli florets
1/2 cauliflower, cut into florets
3/4 cup shredded Gruyère cheese

1 To make the pasta, sift the flour onto a work surface and make a large well in the center in which to place the eggs, olive oil and salt. Using the fingertips of one hand, mix these together and gradually work in the flour until it is all incorporated. The dough should be slightly dry. Knead until smooth and silky. Kneading will result in the elasticity and texture required, so don't add extra liquid. Wrap in plastic wrap and rest for 20 minutes.

2 To make the cheese sauce, melt the butter in a pan, stir in the flour with a wooden spoon and cook gently for 3 minutes, stirring constantly. Remove from the heat and whisk in the cold milk. Blend thoroughly, season with salt and pepper and add the nutmeg. Return to the heat and bring slowly to a boil, stirring constantly. Lower the heat and cook for 7 minutes, stirring occasionally. Stir in the cream and cheese. Set aside, covered with buttered waxed paper.

3 Heat the butter in a skillet and cook the onion slowly without browning. Add the tomatoes, thyme and bay leaf. Season with salt and pepper. Simmer for 15 minutes, or until pulpy. Discard both the bay leaf and the thyme.

4 Bring a large pan of salted water to a boil. Add the carrot, reduce the heat and simmer for 4 minutes. Add the broccoli and cauliflower and simmer for 3 minutes. Drain and refresh in cold water to stop the cooking process. Drain well and set aside.

5 Preheat the oven to 375°F. On a lightly floured surface, roll out the pasta dough to 1/16 inch thick. Cut with a sharp knife into long strips 6 x 3 inches and cook a few strips at a time, in a large pan of boiling salted water with a dash of oil, for 2–3 minutes, or until *al dente*. Transfer to a bowl of cold water, drain and put between layers of a clean dish towel.

6 Mix the cheese sauce and tomato sauce and simmer for 15 minutes. Add the vegetables to the sauce. Season. Butter a 2–2 1/2-quart baking dish and alternate layers of pasta and vegetable mixture, finishing with pasta. Sprinkle cheese over the top and bake for 35 minutes.

Broccoli purée with blue cheese

Puréed broccoli goes well with almost any dish. Add the cheese only moments before serving.

*Preparation time **10 minutes***
*Total cooking time **20 minutes***
Serves 4–6

I head of broccoli
3 tablespoons unsalted butter
1 1/2 oz. blue cheese, shredded or crumbled

1 Trim the individual broccoli stalks from the main stem, discard the stem and check that about 4 cups of broccoli remain. Wash thoroughly and drain, then trim and slice the stalks very thinly, reserving the flower heads.
2 Melt the butter in a medium pan, add the sliced stalks, cover with waxed paper and a lid. Cook very gently for 10 minutes until tender, but not colored. Finely chop the flower heads and add them to the pan with 1/2 cup water. Cook, uncovered, for 5 minutes until tender, but still bright green. Drain well, transfer to a food processor and blend until smooth. Return to the pan, reheat and remove from the heat to stir in the cheese. Season to taste with salt and pepper.
3 Serve the purée as oval quenelle shapes by pushing a rounded soup spoon of purée off the spoon using another spoon, both held horizontally, or simply serve it in a neat mound.

Chef's tip A great accompaniment to meat, fish or poultry, and especially good with steak. Do not add the cheese until just before serving or it may become stringy with overheating.

Carrot purée

For this method of cooking, the carrots should be sliced very thinly so they will cook quickly and evenly.

*Preparation time **10 minutes***
*Total cooking time **20 minutes***
Serves 4–6

3 tablespoons unsalted butter
14 oz. carrots, thinly sliced (about 3 medium)
pinch of nutmeg or ground coriander

1 Melt the butter in a large shallow skillet, add the carrot and season with salt and pepper. Add the nutmeg or coriander. Cover the pan with a sheet of waxed paper and a lid. It is important to cover to prevent loss of steam made by the carrots as they cook, or they will dry and turn brown.
2 Cook over low heat for 15 minutes, or until very soft and tender enough to be mashed with a fork, then remove the paper and lid. Cook, uncovered, over high heat to reduce any excess moisture, then cool slightly. Purée in a food processor until smooth. Return to the pan, adjust the seasoning and reheat to serve.
3 Serve the purée as oval quenelle shapes by pushing a rounded soup spoon of purée off the spoon using another spoon, both held horizontally, or simply serve it in a neat mound.

Chef's tip The purée may be reheated in the microwave as long as it is in a suitable container.

Carrot purée (top) and Broccoli purée with blue cheese

Warm lentil salad with mustard vinaigrette

This traditional regional salad, high in protein, may be served with shellfish, such as shrimp. Normally, the small French Puy lentils are used as they hold their shape well. However, other lentils with the same qualities could be substituted for these. Red lentils are not suitable as they soften to a purée.

*Preparation time **15 minutes + overnight soaking***
*Total cooking time **40 minutes***
Serves 6

1¹/2 cups brown or green lentils
3 tablespoons unsalted butter
2/3 cup diced carrots
¹/2 onion, diced
3 oz. bacon, diced
1¹/4 cups chicken stock (see page 63)
1 butterhead lettuce

VINAIGRETTE
2 tablespoons coarse-grain mustard
2 teaspoons white wine vinegar
¹/3 cup olive or peanut oil
¹/4 cup chopped fresh parsley

1 Soak the lentils in cold water overnight. Drain.
2 Melt the butter in a large saucepan, add the vegetables and bacon and cook gently until the vegetables are soft, but not brown. Add the lentils and chicken stock to the saucepan. Cover and simmer very gently for 30–35 minutes, or until the lentils are tender. Season with salt and pepper.
3 Pour the mixture into a sieve to drain off the liquid. Transfer the lentils, vegetables and the bacon to a large bowl.
4 To make the vinaigrette, place the mustard and vinegar in a bowl and whisk to combine. Season with salt and freshly ground black pepper and very slowly add the olive or peanut oil, whisking constantly. Finally, add the parsley.
5 Toss the warm lentils, vegetables and bacon with the vinaigrette. Arrange a bed of lettuce leaves on a plate and pile the warm salad in the center.

Vegetables in white wine

Experiment with different vegetables to see which you prefer. Make this dish according to the traditional recipe below, or vary it with an oriental touch or your favorite herbs.

*Preparation time **1 hour***
*Total cooking time **50 minutes***
Serves 4

2¹/₂ tablespoons olive oil
3 oz. bacon, cut into strips
3 shallots, finely chopped
I large carrot, cut into batons (see page 63)
I stalk celery, cut into batons
¹/₂ fennel bulb, cut into batons
¹/₃ cup white wine
¹/₃ cup chicken stock (see page 63)
   or water
2 large tomatoes, peeled, seeded
   and diced (see page 62)
²/₃ cup shelled fresh peas
3 oz. green beans,
   trimmed and cut into short lengths
¹/₃ cup toasted pine nuts (pignola)

1 In a large skillet, heat the oil over medium heat and cook the bacon until golden brown. Lower the heat, add the shallots and a pinch of salt. Cook for 2 minutes, without coloring. Add the carrot, celery, fennel and a pinch of salt, and cook gently for 5 minutes.

2 Add the white wine and chicken stock and cook over medium heat until almost dry. Add the tomatoes and cook for 5–10 minutes, or until tender.

3 In two separate saucepans, cook the peas and green beans in boiling salted water for 8–10 minutes, or until tender. Drain and refresh in iced water until completely cooled. Drain well and add to the other vegetables. Leave to simmer for 3–5 minutes, or until hot, and season with salt and pepper to taste. Just before serving, sprinkle with toasted pine nuts. Serve hot or cold.

Chef's tip Slow cooking is a must when preparing this dish, in order to keep it moist. For a more oriental flavor, add toasted sesame seeds instead of the pine nuts and use a little soy sauce instead of salt.

Chef's techniques

◆

Preparing tomatoes

Many recipes call for peeled, seeded tomatoes. It is an easy process if you follow these instructions.

Using a very sharp knife, score a small cross in the base of each tomato.

Blanch the tomatoes in a large pan of boiling water for 10 seconds. Remove and plunge into a bowl of ice cold water to stop the cooking and keep the flesh firm.

Pull away the skin from the cross, and discard the skins.

If a recipe calls for the removal of the tomato seeds, cut the tomato in half and use a teaspoon to gently scoop out the seeds.

Preparing whole artichokes

You can cook either the whole artichoke, as shown below, or just the heart. Both are delicious.

Break off the artichoke stalk at the bottom, pulling out the fibers that attach it to the base.

Pull off the outer leaves and place the artichoke in a pan of boiling salted water with the juice of 1 lemon. Weigh down with a plate and simmer for 20–35 minutes.

Test for doneness by pulling at one of the leaves. If it comes away easily, the artichoke is done. Cut off the top half of the artichoke and discard.

Remove the hairy choke in the middle of the artichoke with a spoon. The artichoke bottom is now ready to fill.

Clarifying butter

Removing the water and solids from butter makes it less likely to burn. Ghee is a form of clarified butter.

To make about $^1/_3$ cup clarified butter, cut 6 oz. butter into small cubes. Place in a small pan set into a larger pot of water over low heat. Melt the butter, without stirring.

Remove the pan from the heat and allow to cool slightly. Skim the foam from the surface, being careful not to stir the butter.

Pour off the clear yellow liquid, being very careful to leave the milky sediment behind in the pan. Discard the sediment and store the clarified butter in an airtight container in the refrigerator.

Making chicken stock

Good, flavorsome homemade stock can be the cornerstone of a great dish.

Cut up 1 $^1/_2$ lb. chicken bones and carcass and put in a pan with a coarsely chopped onion, carrot and celery stalk. Add 6 peppercorns, a bouquet garni and 4 quarts cold water.

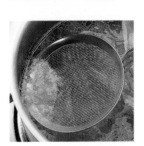

Bring to a boil and let the stock simmer gently for 2–3 hours, skimming off any scum that rises to the surface using a large spoon. Strain the stock through a sieve into a clean bowl, then allow to cool.

Chill the stock overnight, then lift off any fat. If you can't leave overnight, drag the surface of the hot strained stock with paper towels to lift off the fat. Makes 6–8 cups.

Baton vegetables

Evenly sized vegetables cook uniformly and look attractive in dishes such as ratatouille.

Use a long, very sharp knife to cut the vegetables into batons.

Washing leeks

Leeks are often used in cooking as they impart a unique flavor.

Before use, leeks need to be rinsed thoroughly under cold running water to dislodge and remove all traces of dirt or grit. Slit the green tops to help the water run through the tightly furled leaves.

First published in the United States in 1998 by Periplus Editions (HK) Ltd., with editorial offices at
153 Milk Street, Boston, Massachusetts 02109.

Murdoch Books and Le Cordon Bleu thank the 32 masterchefs of all the Le Cordon Bleu Schools, whose knowledge and
expertise have made this book possible, especially: Chef Cliche (MOF), Chef Terrien, Chef Boucheret, Chef Duchêne (MOF),
Chef Guillut, Chef Steneck, Paris; Chef Males, Chef Walsh, Chef Hardy, London; Chef Chantefort, Chef Bertin, Chef Jambert,
Chef Honda, Tokyo; Chef Salembien, Chef Boutin, Chef Harris, Sydney; Chef Lawes, Adelaide; Chef Guiet, Chef Denis, Ottawa.
Of the many people who helped the Chefs test each recipe, a special mention to David Welch and Allen Wertheim.
A very special acknowledgment to Directors Susan Eckstein, Great Britain, and Kathy Shaw, Paris, who have been responsible for
the coordination of the Le Cordon Bleu team throughout this series.

The Publisher and Le Cordon Bleu also wish to thank Carole Sweetnam for her help with this series.

First published in Australia in 1998 by Murdoch Books®

Managing Editor: Kay Halsey
Series Concept, Design and Art Direction: Juliet Cohen
Editor: Wendy Stephen
Food Director: Jody Vassallo
Food Editors: Lulu Grimes, Tracy Rutherford
US Editor: Linda Venturoni Wilson
Designer: Marylouise Brammer
Photographers: Joe Filshie, Chris Jones
Food Stylists: Carolyn Fienberg, Mary Harris
Food Preparation: Jo Forrest, Kerrie Ray
Chef's Techniques Photographer: Reg Morrison
Home Economists: Michelle Lawton, Kerrie Mullins, Justine Poole, Kerrie Ray

Library of Congress catalog card number: 98-65441
ISBN 962-593-433-2

Front cover, from top: Provençal stuffed tomatoes; Mixed glazed vegetables; Green beans with bacon.

Distributed in the United States by
Charles E. Tuttle Co., Inc.
RR1 Box 231-5
North Clarendon, VT 05759
Tel: (802) 773-8930
Fax: (802) 773-6993

Printed in Singapore

05 04 03 02 01 00 99 98   10 9 8 7 6 5 4 3 2 1

Important: Some of the recipes in this book may include raw eggs, which can cause salmonella poisoning.
Those who might be at risk from this (the elderly, pregnant women, young children and those suffering
from immune deficiency diseases) should check with their physicians before eating raw eggs.